★ WHEN ★
Amelia Earhart
═ BUILT A ═
ROLLER COASTER

by Mark Weakland

illustrated by Oksana Grivina

PICTURE WINDOW BOOKS
a capstone imprint

*A*melia Earhart was different than other girls of her day. She loved action and adventure. Instead of wearing dresses while she played, she wore pants. She loved running along the bluffs near the Missouri River. And instead of dreaming of marriage and a family, Amelia dreamed of flying.

Amelia Earhart became one of America's best-known aviators. She was an inspiration to women everywhere. But she started out just like you—a fun-loving kid.

Amelia was born July 24, 1897. Right from the start, she was pumping her little arms and legs!

Her sister Muriel was born almost two and a half years later. Because Muriel couldn't say "Amelia," she called her sister "Meely." Amelia called Muriel "Pidge."

Both girls were rough and tumble tomboys. Their mother, Amy, encouraged their outdoor activity.

"I don't believe in bringing up 'nice little girls' who only play with dolls and wear dresses," she said. She had blue gym suits sewn for them so they could race, jump, and climb trees, just like the boys.

Amelia and Muriel did not care for dolls. But they each had a favorite toy. Amelia's was a wooden donkey. "I'll call you Donk," she said.

Muriel's favorite toy was an elephant named Ellie. Donk and Ellie followed the girls everywhere.

Amelia always wanted to do what boys did. One year she asked her father for a football. He bought two, one for each of his daughters.

"Throw one to Donk!" cried Amelia as Muriel got ready to toss the ball.

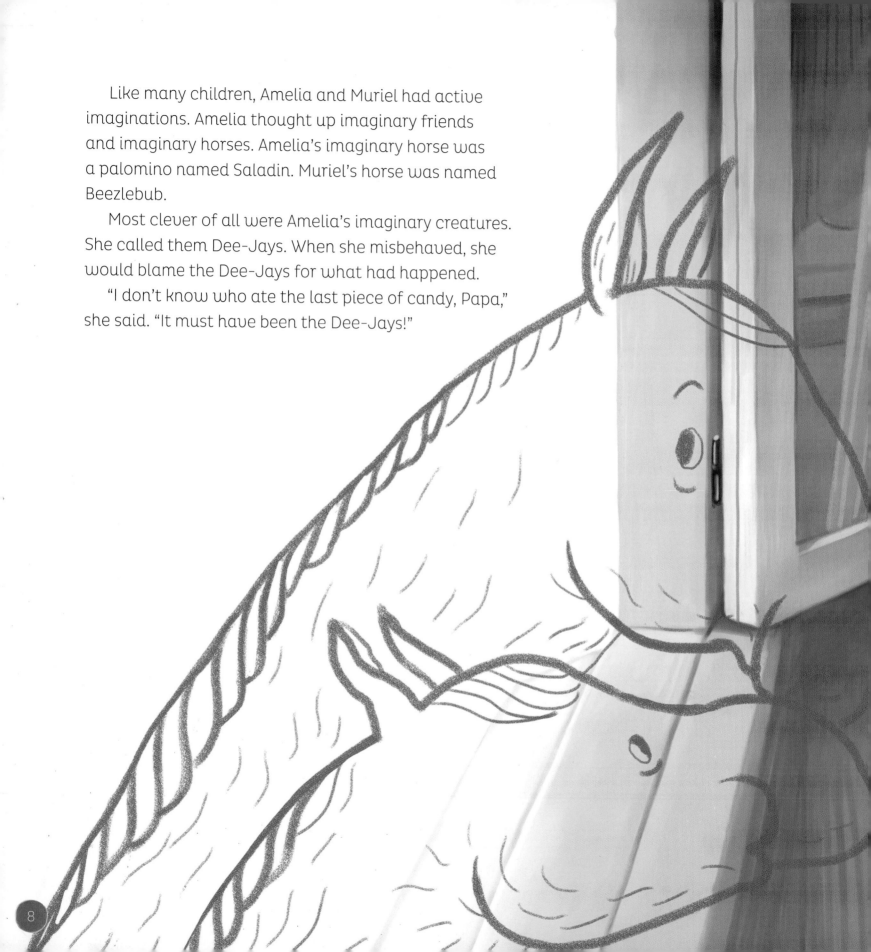

Like many children, Amelia and Muriel had active imaginations. Amelia thought up imaginary friends and imaginary horses. Amelia's imaginary horse was a palomino named Saladin. Muriel's horse was named Beezlebub.

Most clever of all were Amelia's imaginary creatures. She called them Dee-Jays. When she misbehaved, she would blame the Dee-Jays for what had happened.

"I don't know who ate the last piece of candy, Papa," she said. "It must have been the Dee-Jays!"

One Christmas Amelia got a sled. At that time a girl's sled was like a chair. To ride it, a girl had to sit up. But Amelia got a boy's sled, long and low to the ground.

"It will be perfect for belly whopping!" she cried.

At the top of the hill one day, Amelia "belly slammed" to get started, just like the boys. As she zoomed down the hill, a horse-drawn cart pulled right in front of her. In a split second, Amelia had slid between the legs of the horse!

Amelia laughed. **"Had I been sitting up, either my head or the horse's ribs would have suffered in contact—probably the horse's ribs,"** she said.

Amelia loved mechanical things. Her most famous creation was a roller coaster. The track was made of boards greased with lard. The car was an empty wooden crate. With a little help, Amelia climbed into the crate and launched herself down the track. At the end, the car flew into the air and crashed to the ground!

Amelia was too excited to be hurt. "Oh, Pidge," she cried. "It's just like flying!"

Amelia also loved adventure, even if it was imaginary. Her grandmother's barn was the perfect place for such thrills. She and Pidge, along with some cousins, would climb into an old carriage in the barn. Together the group went on many wild and exciting trips, without ever really leaving that barn.

"Giddy-yap, old girl," Amelia yelled. "Those bandits are hot on our trail!"

"Yee-haw!" cried Muriel.

As a child Amelia learned to stay calm, even in scary situations. She had a large black dog named James Ferocious. One day some boys teased him. Lunging and snarling, James broke his chain and chased the boys. They scrambled to the top of a shed for safety.

Amelia heard the boys yelling and came running to help. "James Ferocious, you naughty dog," she said in a soothing voice. "You've tipped over your water dish. Come along and I'll get you some more."

This did the trick. James trotted after Amelia into the house.

Amelia was not only calm. She was brave too. Muriel and Amelia sometimes traveled with their parents by train. During one trip it rained and rained. The land near the train began flooding.

As the train inched along, some passengers began to panic.

Seeing the water, Muriel turned to her sister and asked, "Are you afraid, Meely?"

"Of course not," replied Amelia.

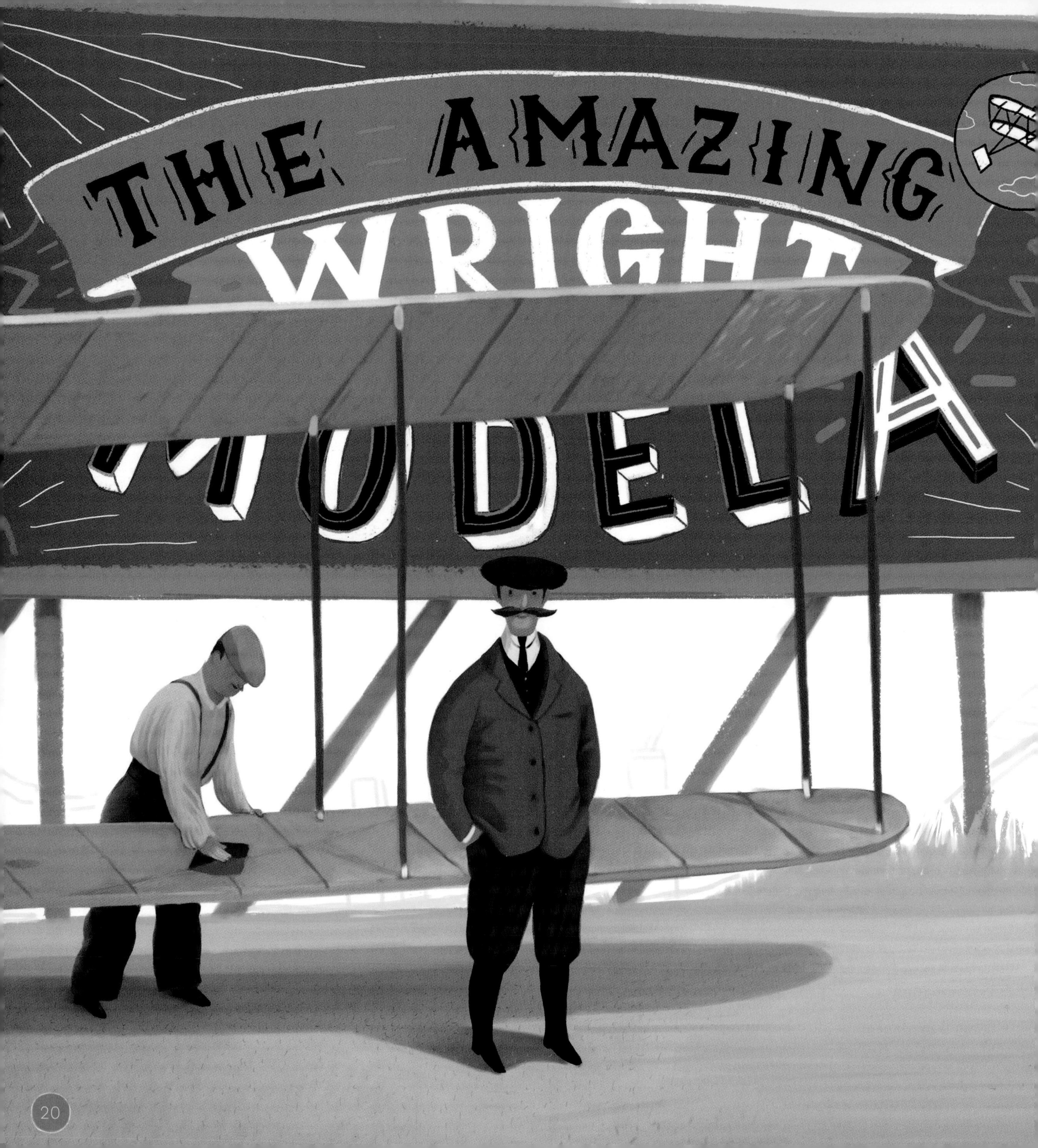
THE AMAZING
WRIGHT
MODEL A

Amelia saw her first airplane when she was 10 years old. The first airplane flight had taken place just a few years before, and the airplane Amelia saw was a simple-looking machine.

"It's a thing of rusty wire and wood," she noted. "It's not at all interesting."

Little did Amelia know that 10 years later, she would make airplanes the focus of her life.

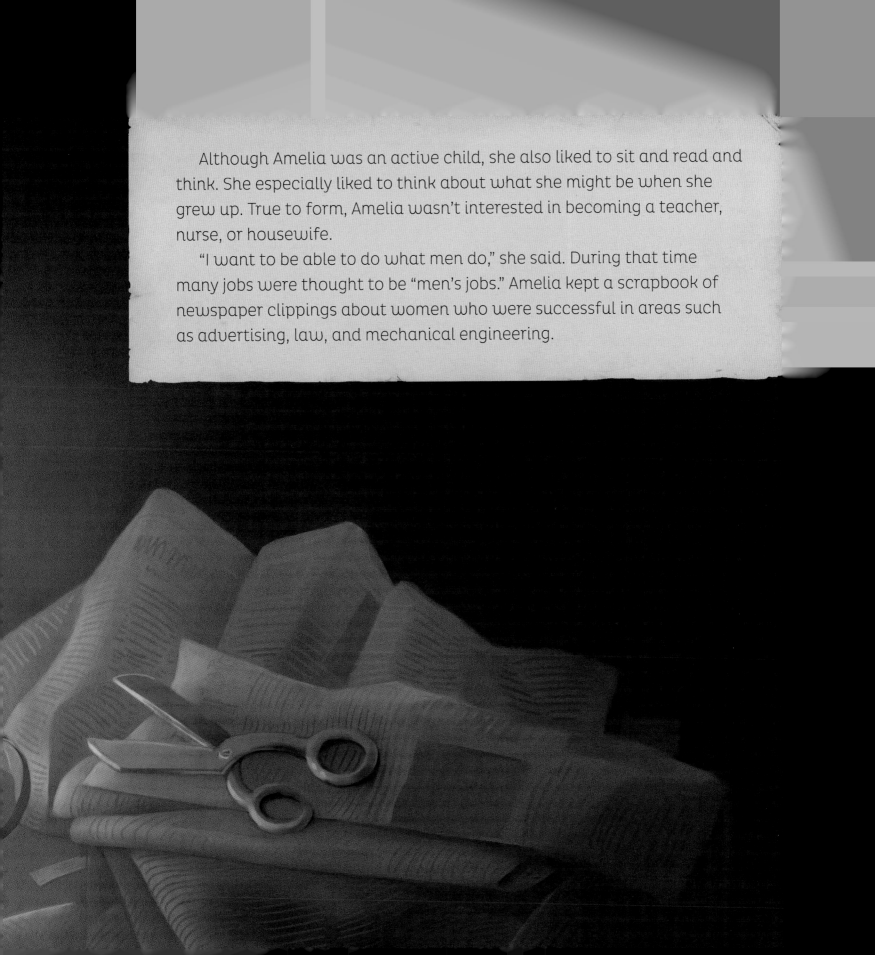

Although Amelia was an active child, she also liked to sit and read and think. She especially liked to think about what she might be when she grew up. True to form, Amelia wasn't interested in becoming a teacher, nurse, or housewife.

"I want to be able to do what men do," she said. During that time many jobs were thought to be "men's jobs." Amelia kept a scrapbook of newspaper clippings about women who were successful in areas such as advertising, law, and mechanical engineering.

As a grown woman, Amelia did things that women never had. She took flying lessons. And she bought her own plane, which she named *The Canary*.

Amelia was picked to be the first female passenger on a transatlantic flight.

Soon after, her flying career took off. She flew regularly, entered races, and spoke to others about flying. Amelia's husband, George Putnam, organized her flights and scheduled the public talks she gave.

25

NEWFOUNDLAND

In 1932 Amelia became the first woman to fly solo across the Atlantic Ocean. It was a tough trip—more than 2,000 miles (3,219 kilometers) long. Amelia grew tired during the journey. The plane's fuel tank leaked. At one point flames shot out of the engine! But that didn't rattle Amelia.

IRELAND

Atlantic Ocean

Almost 15 hours after Amelia had started, she landed in Ireland. Her transatlantic flight was a historic achievement. Amelia had become one of the greatest aviators in the world. Although many of her journeys were difficult, she never lost the fun-loving, can-do attitude she had as a child.

AFTERWORD

For years Amelia had dreamed of flying along Earth's equator until she had circled the globe. In June 1937 she set out to accomplish this dream. By July she had traveled more than 22,000 miles (35,406 km). But on July 2, 1937, Amelia vanished, along with her navigator Fred Noonan. It is most likely that she ran out of fuel while looking for her landing site. For days the U.S. government searched for Amelia and Fred. But they were never found.

Amelia Earhart led by being an example to others. As a child she showed a determination to be herself. And as she grew older, she stayed true to what she believed.

"Women must try to do things as men have tried," she said. "When they fail, their failure must be but a challenge to others."

Today people are still inspired by Amelia Earhart's life of bravery and accomplishment.

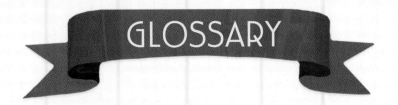

GLOSSARY

aviator—a person who flies an aircraft

bluff—a tall, steep bank or cliff

engineering—using science to design and build things

equator—an imaginary line around the middle of Earth; it divides the Northern and Southern Hemispheres

ferocious—wild and fierce

imagination—the ability to form pictures in your mind of things that are not present or real

inspire—to influence or encourage people in a good way

mechanical—having to do with machines or tools

palomino—a horse with a golden coat and white mane and tail

transatlantic—crossing or reaching across the Atlantic ocean

vanish—to disappear

READ MORE

Gilpin, Caroline Crosson. *Amelia Earhart*. National Geographic Readers. Washington, D.C.: National Geographic, 2013.

Mara, Wil. *Amelia Earhart*. Rookie Biographies. New York: Children's Press, and imprint of Scholastic Inc., 2014.

Meltzer, Brad. *I am Amelia Earhart*. Ordinary People Change the World. New York: Dial Books for Young Readers, an imprint of Penguin Group Inc., 2014.

CRITICAL THINKING WITH THE
— COMMON CORE —

1 A child's actions often indicate the type of adult he or she will become. What did Amelia Earhart do as a child that indicated what kind of adult she would become? Provide two examples and support your answer with words from the text. (Key Ideas and Details)

2 Did Amelia's family try to help her become an active and independent person, or did they try to stop her from becoming an active and independent person? Support your answer with two pieces of evidence from the text. (Integration of Knowledge and Ideas)

3 The author says that Amelia Earhart believed "… it is better to try and fail then never to try at all." What evidence in the book supports this claim? Provide two examples from the book that support this statement. (Craft and Structure)

INTERNET SITES

FactHound offers a safe, fun way to find Internet sites
related to this book. All of the sites on FactHound
have been researched by our staff.

Here's all you do:

Visit www.facthound.com

Type in this code: 9781479596867

Super-cool stuff!

Check out projects, games, and lots more at
www.capstonekids.com

OTHER TITLES IN ★ THIS SERIES ★

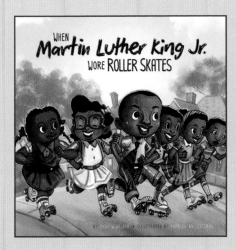

INDEX

airplanes, 21, 24

Dee-Jays, 8
Donk, 6

Earhart, Amelia
  birth, 5
  bravery of, 19
  disappearance of, 28
  flying lessons, 24
  transatlantic flights, 25, 27

Earhart, Muriel, 5, 6

football, 6

James Ferocious, 16

Putnam, George, 25

roller coasters, 13

Saladin, 8
sleds, 11

Special thanks to our adviser for her advice and expertise:
Michelle Cervone, Amelia Earhart Historian

Editor: Shelly Lyons
Designer: Russell Griesmer
Creative Director: Nathan Gassman
Production Specialist: Tori Abraham
The illustrations in this book were created digitally.

Note from the Editor: Direct quotations in the main text are indicated by **bold** words.

Direct Quotations are found on the following pages:
page 11, line 9: Earhart, Amelia. *The Fun of It*: *Random Records of My Own Flying
and of Women in Aviation*. Chicago: Academy Press, 1977, p. 12.
page 19, line 7: Earhart Morrissey, Muriel. *Amelia, My Courageous Sister*.
Santa Clara, Calif.: Osborne Publisher, 1987, page 24.
page 28, line 10: Earhart, Amelia. *Last Flight*. New York: Orion Books, [1988], 1937, p. 134.

Picture Window Books are published by Capstone, 1710 Roe Crest Drive, North Mankato, Minnesota 56003
www.mycapstone.com

Library of Congress Cataloging-in-Publication Data
Names: Weakland, Mark. | Grivina, Oksana, illustrator.
Title: When Amelia Earhart built a roller coaster / by Mark Weakland ; illustrated by Oksana Grivina.
Description: North Mankato, Minnesota : Picture Window Books, 2017. | Series: Leaders doing headstands Audience: Grades 4 to 6. |
Includes bibliographical references and index.
Identifiers: LCCN 2015050707
ISBN 9781479596867 (library binding)
ISBN 9781515801382 (paperback)
ISBN 9781515801467 (eBook PDF)
Subjects: LCSH: Earhart, Amelia, 1897-1937—Childhood and youth—Juvenile literature. | Women air pilots—United States—
Biography—Juvenile literature. | Air pilots—United States—Biography—Juvenile literature.
Classification: LCC TL540.E3 W425 2017 | DDC 629.13092—dc23
LC record available at http://lccn.loc.gov/2015050707

Printed in the United States of America in North Mankato, Minnesota.
112017   010948R